Get the
Duck

by Sarah Snashall

illustrated by Annabel Tempest

OXFORD
UNIVERSITY PRESS

Mum gets the tickets.

Sam is in a sack.

Dad tugs and Tess pulls.

Get the duck, Tess.

6

Get the duck, Sam.

7

Run up, Dad.

It is a miss.

It is a mess.

No! It is a picnic.

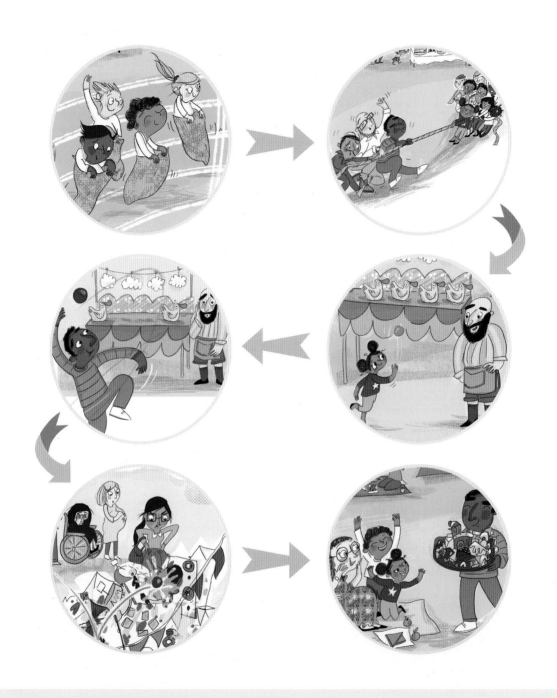

 Encourage the child to use the pictures to retell the story.